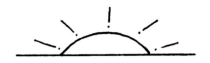

A special dedication of thanks to my mentors
and educational institutions.
In Philadelphia PA. they include: Rowan Elementary,
Roosevelt Middle School, Germantown High School
and in Pittsburgh, the Art Institute of Pittsburgh.

Also in Philadelphia a special personal thanks to the staff
and faculty of Temples, Small Business Development Center for providing
me with their service and expertise.

Copyright © 2006 by Dwayne Henson.   574381

ISBN: Softcover   978-1-4257-0083-6
         Hardcover   978-1-4257-4427-4
         EBook   978-1-4691-2848-1

Print information available on the last page

Rev. date: 03/27/2019

To order additional copies of this book, contact:
Xlibris
1-888-795-4274
www.Xlibris.com
Orders@Xlibris.com

Discover the inspirational magic created from
smiles through the guidance of Mr. Sunny Sunshine.

"Jump start!"
Written and illustrated
by
Dwayne S. Henson

Hello! Hello! It's Mr. Sunny Sunshine and I've traveled happily far on my way on a rainbow today to help you jump start your school day. As I lead you on your way there's lots of positive advice to share and many encouraging lessons to learn that will help guide you towards educational success and achievement.

"So let's get jump started!"

School

Ring! Ring! Ring! Listen up; school is where you can get a great opportunity to gain a good education. An education can help lead you onto a path towards opportunity, success, and achievement with lots of smiles.

School

Going through school and getting a good education can be a fun learning experience, that you can look back on and be proud of your educational rewards and achievements with plenty of smiles.

Reading:

Don't just leap over a book for fun and smiles. Reading can also be a fun learning experience that you can enjoy throughout your life.

Give that extra, extra, effort in making it onto the top with a smile. To achieve high honors it takes lots of hard work and extra effort.

honors

Smile and always do your very best and strive for the highest of honors.

Looking for a clue to educational achievement and success? Study! Study! Study! That will always make a smiling difference.

Listen

Listen, smile, and learn! Good listening skills are a very important key to learning

While you're in school it's important to focus in on learning. Make it a good habit like smiling.

Learning

To climb the ladder of higher learning, when setting your goals aim real high. There's always another step to climb. Keep smiling and always keep learning.

Tardiness

Don't be late for school; try to make that a golden rule. Also don't forget to smile, smile, smile while you're on the way, that's always a good way to start off your day!

While you're in school there's a special time and place for having fun. Recess is that special time to meet lots of other smiling faces having fun too.

Recess

Good, better, best smile and never settle for less. Try to make good even better and better your very best!

Practice makes perfect.

To achieve excellence in all that you set out to do you must practice, practice, practice and a little smiling always help too.

Here are a few valuable
lessons to remember
as you journey along.

Smile and always remember that patience is a virtue. No one learns to fly overnight.

To enjoy the smiles of success, you must always take one step at a time. No matter how you do it. Remember that it's always one step at a time.

In your daily journey through life never stop smiling or learning! There's always a lesson to be learned...

I think I'm learning one now. Keep smiling!

A lesson that you can
be sure of... what goes around
come around. Smile and be kind to
others and others will smile and
be kind to you.

Let the beauty within your heart shine bright on the outside with a happy bright smile.

A lesson to remember.

Honesty can carry you
a long, long, way. Keep
smiling and believing in
honesty as you journey on.

I sure hope you enjoyed "Jump start!" today. It was certainly my pleasure to share with you a few valuable lessons and some encouraging advice that will help guide you along on your way as you start your school day. So long for now and enjoy your school day.

Next a special offer and a preview of more up coming Mr. Sunny Sunshine™ books. ⟶

A special offer from
the author / illustrator of the
Mr. Sunny Sunshine books
Dwayne S. Henson

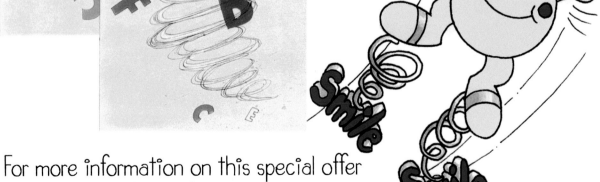

Here's my special offer.
Two preschool educational
books combined in one at
one regular sales price.

For more information on this special offer
and other Mr. Sunny Sunshine books
Contact Xlibris at: 1-888-795-4274

Dwayne S. Henson
Creator of Mr. Sunny Sunshine™

My gift that I would like to share with others is to inspire those who are in need of a smile and to educate others of the positive inspirational value that smiles provide in our society.

With Mr. Sunny Sunshine™ as my tool in this never ending educational smile-based journey, I aim to demonstrate how smiles can be utilized in so many positive encouraging ways such as to inspire, motivate, educate as well as to entertain. How Mr. Sunny Sunshine™ creates smiles and shares them with others, I truly believe, are some of the fascinating trademark dynamics of this inspiring smile making concept.

As you may come to discover there's more inspirational magic behind a smile than what we generally see.

From this unique unit of books you'll learn how and why Mr. Sunny Sunshine™ took it upon himself to create more smiles and inspiration all over the world. Along with this you'll also be provided with a one-of-a-kind, entertaining, smile-based education and much, much, more.

There's a lot to uncover and learn about a smile. I invite you to journey along to see how truly motivating a smile can be.

I certainly hope you enjoy my Mr. Sunny Sunshine™ books as much as I did creating them for others to share. I look forward to creating lots more smiles for many of years to come.

Sincerely, Dwayne S. Henson... Prince of happiness, King of smiles.

Printed in the United States
By Bookmasters